PLAY GUITAR WITH U2
(1980-1983)

PLAY GUITAR WITH U2
(1980-1983)

ISBN 0-634-09251-0

HAL•LEONARD®
CORPORATION
7777 W. BLUEMOUND RD. P.O. BOX 13819 MILWAUKEE, WI 53213

Visit Hal Leonard Online at
www.halleonard.com

Compiled by Nick Crispin
Music arranged by Arthur Dick
Music processed by Paul Ewers Music Design
Project Editor: Tom Fleming
Printed in Great Britain

CD recorded, mixed and mastered by Jonas Persson
All guitars by Arthur Dick
Bass by Paul Townsend
Drums by Brett Morgan

Out Of Control

Words & Music by U2

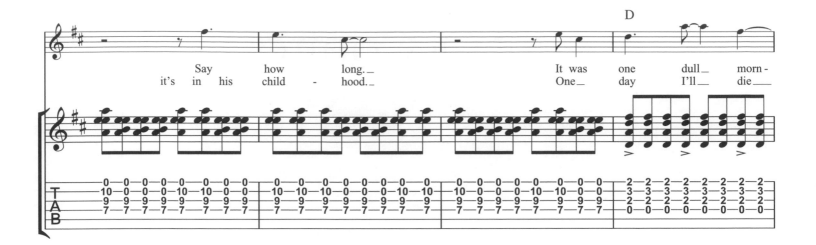

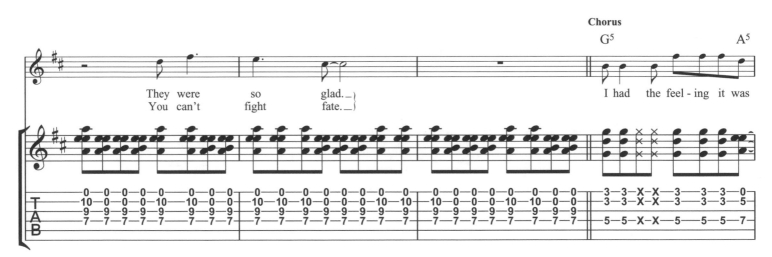

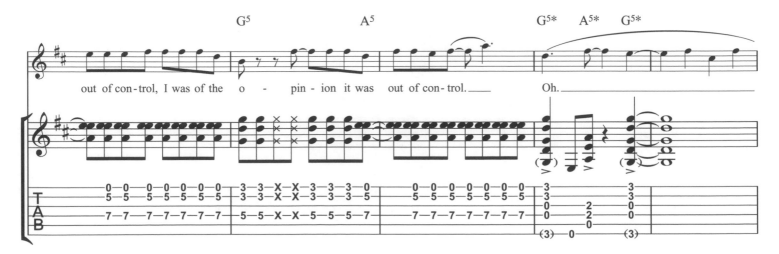

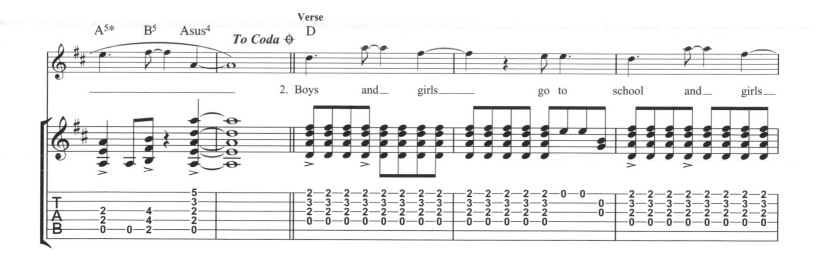

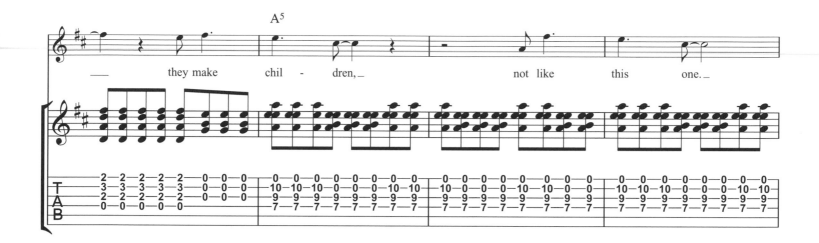

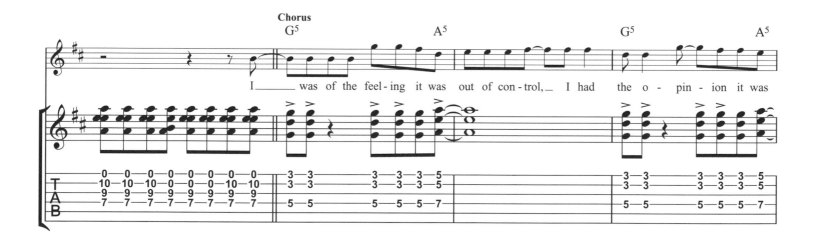

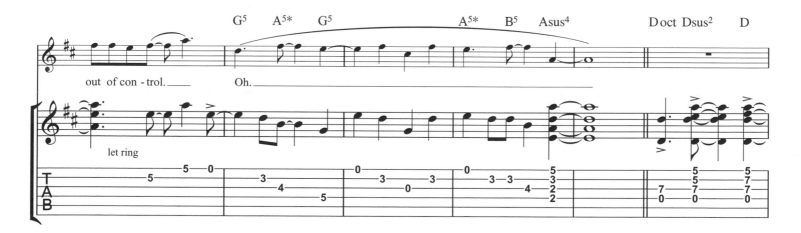

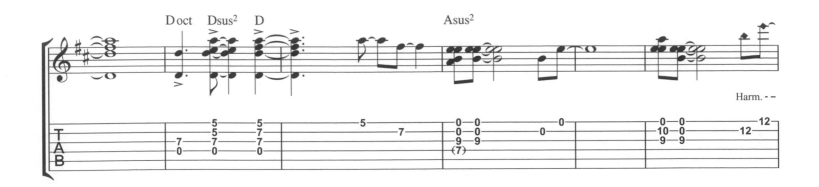

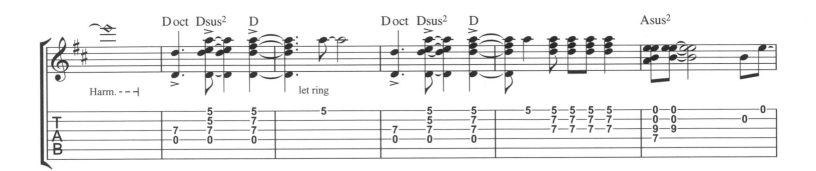

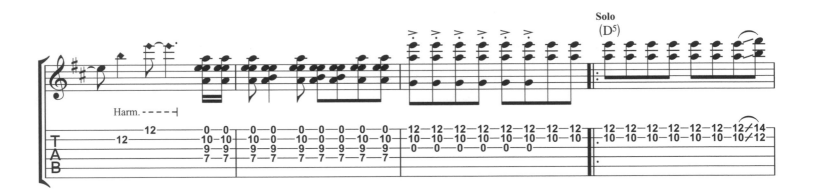

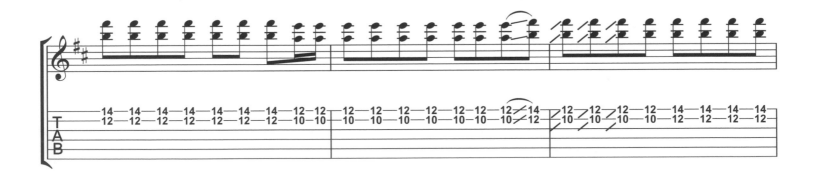

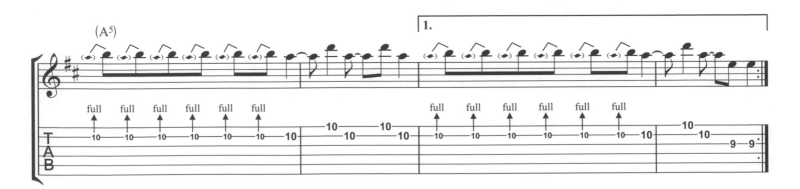

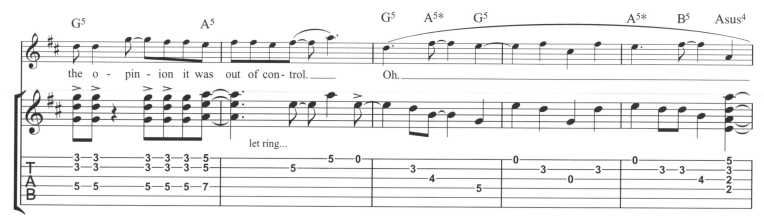

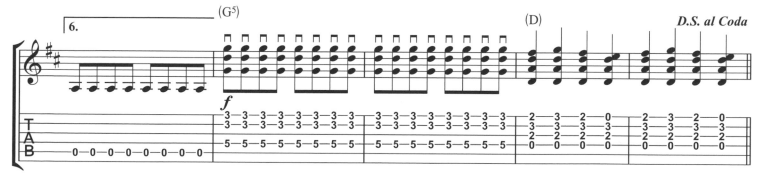

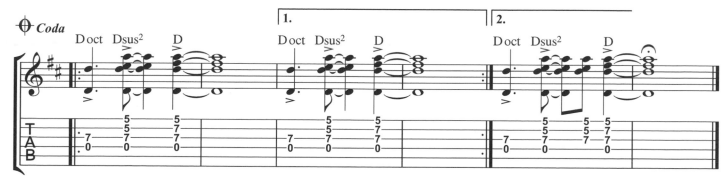

I Will Follow

Words & Music by U2

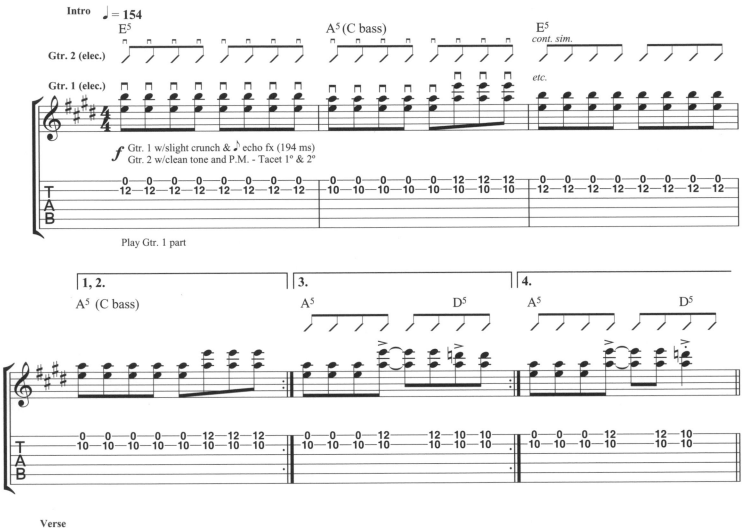

Tune guitars down a semitone

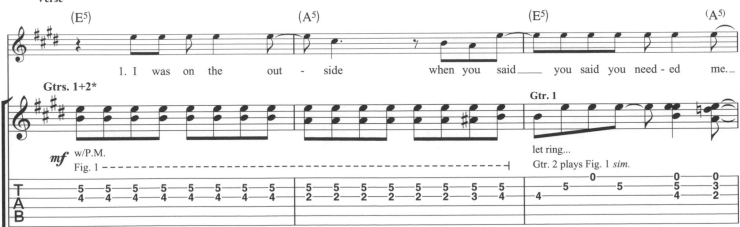

* combined part, Gtr. 2 plays same part at 9th position (see chord boxes)

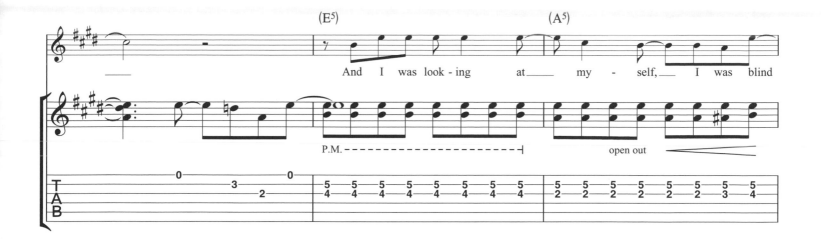

And I was look-ing at my-self, I was blind

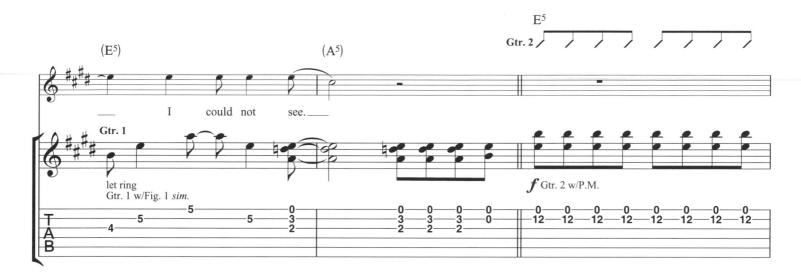

I could not see.

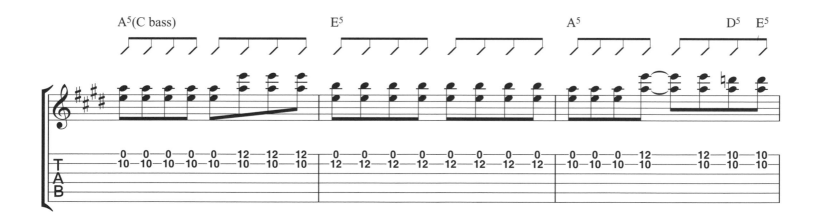

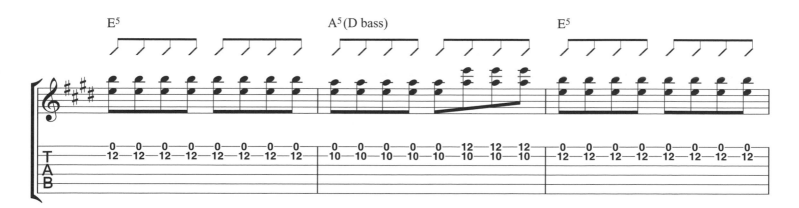

13

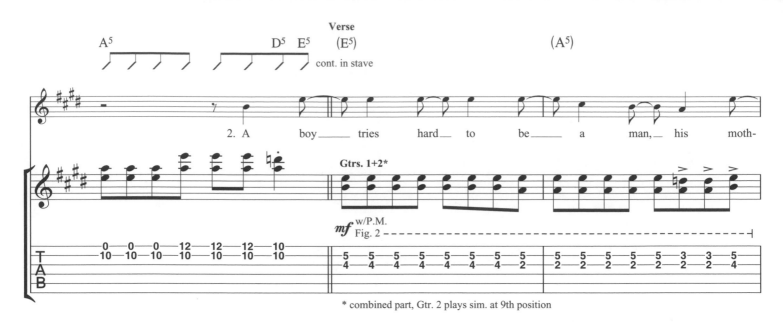

* combined part, Gtr. 2 plays sim. at 9th position

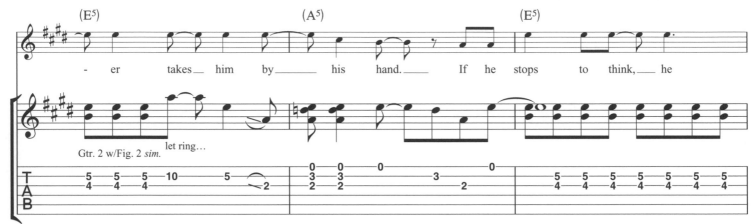

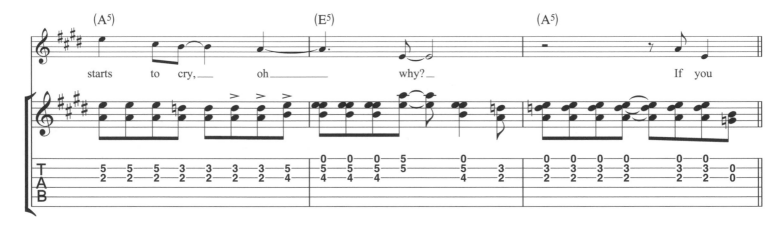

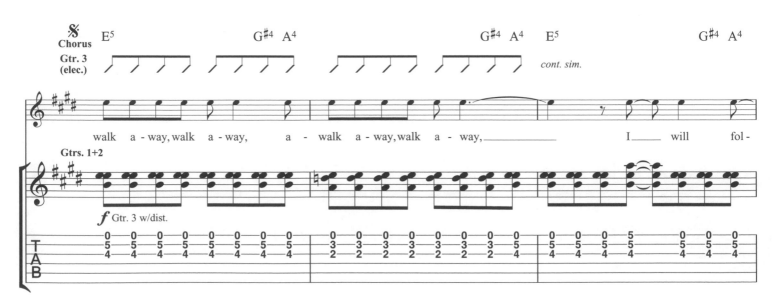

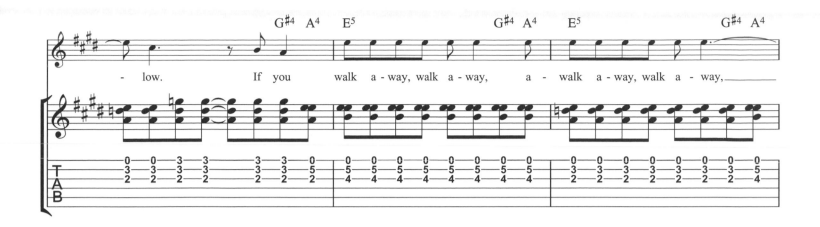

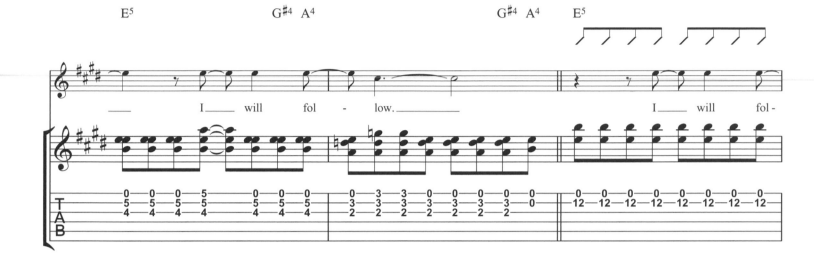

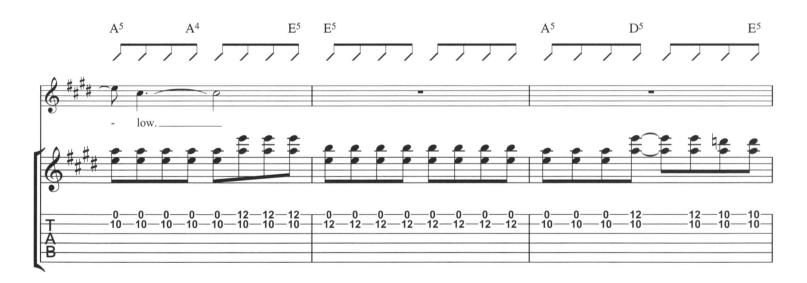

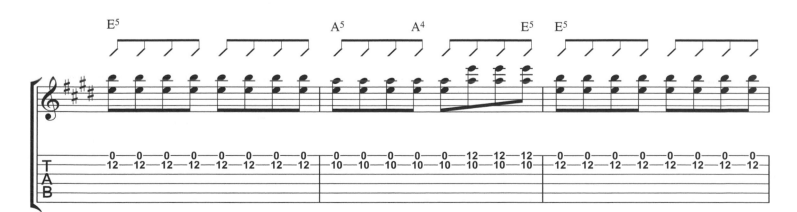

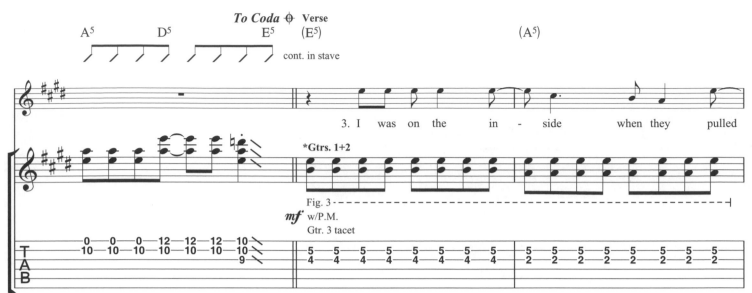

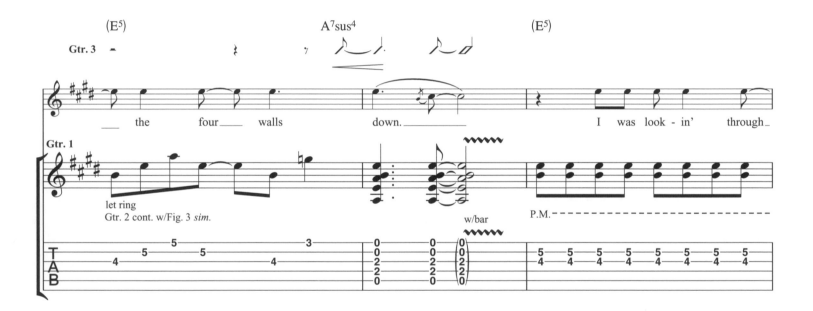

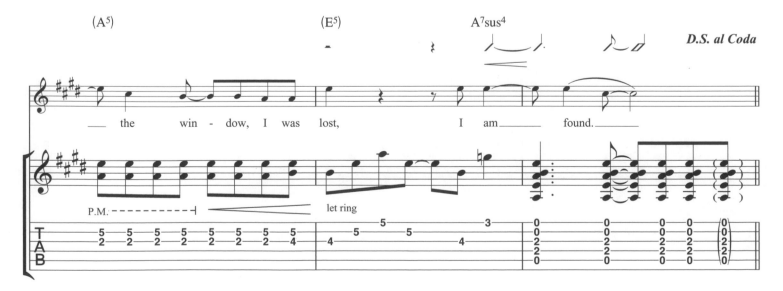

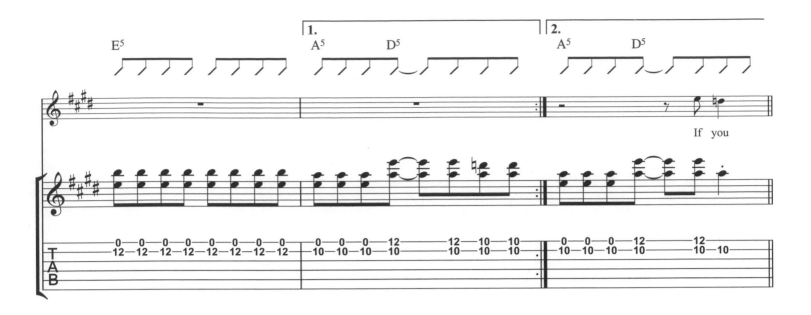

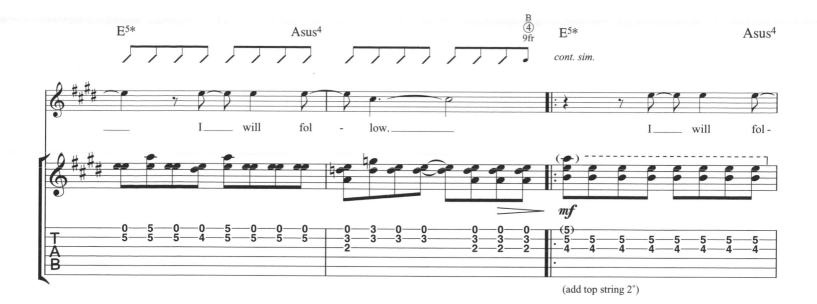

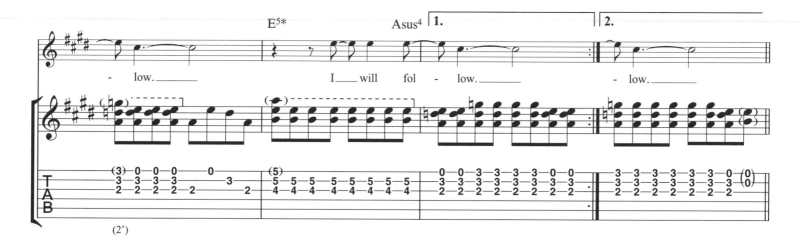

(add top string 2°)

(2°)

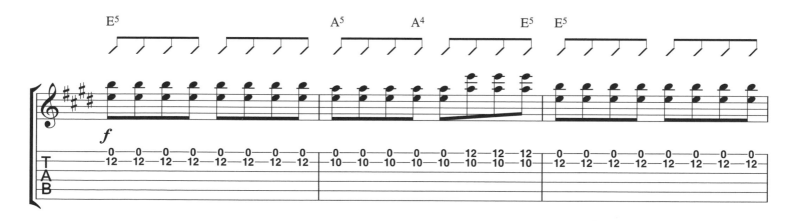

The Electric Co.

Words & Music by U2

Tune all guitars down a semitone

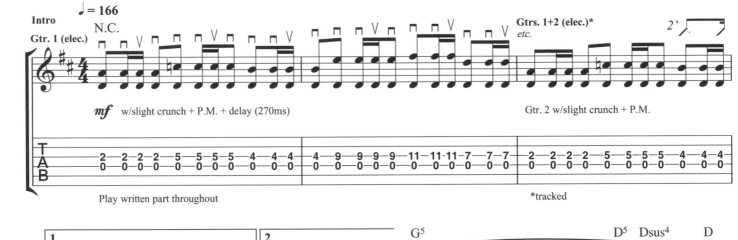

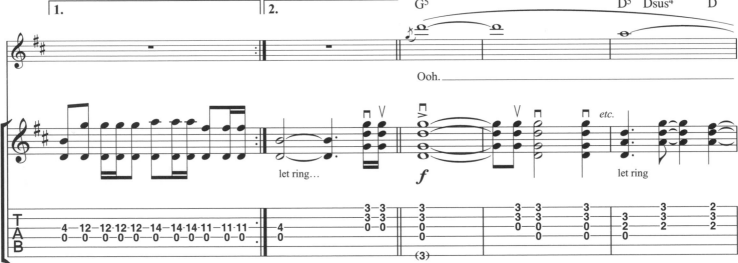

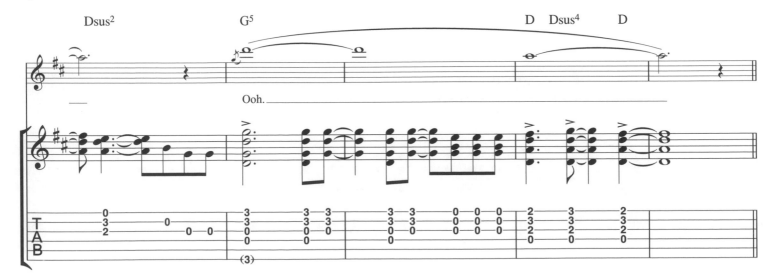

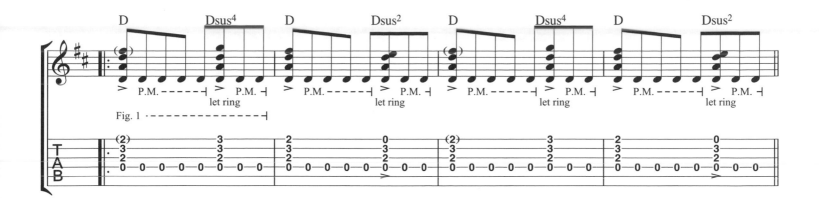

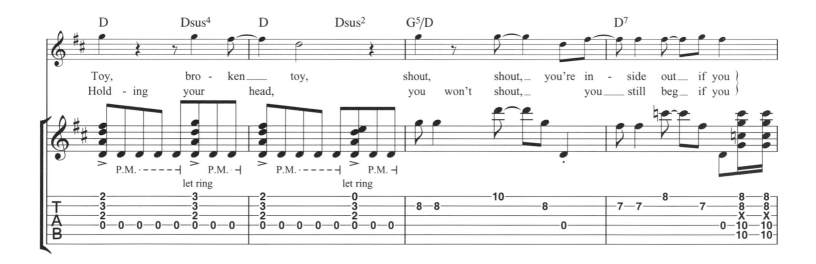

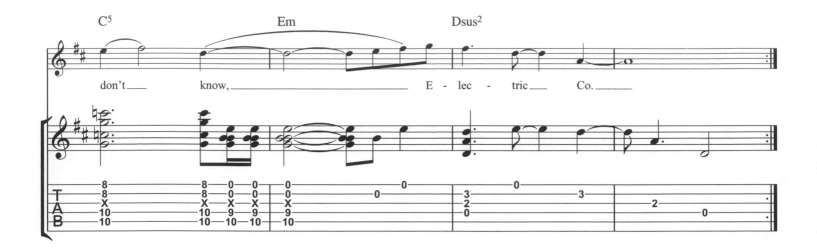

don't _____ know, _____ E - lec - tric ___ Co. _____

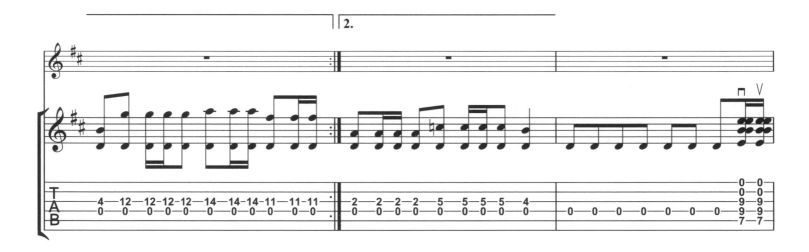

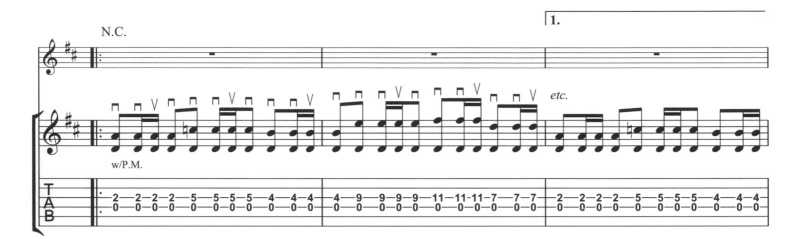

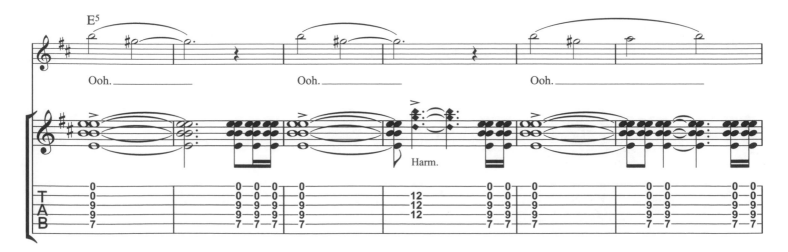

Ooh. _____ Ooh. _____ Ooh. _____

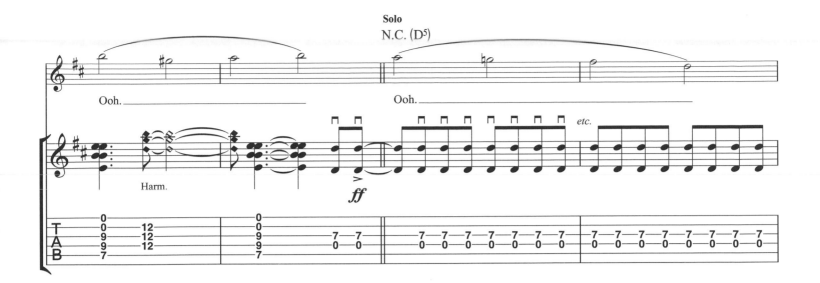

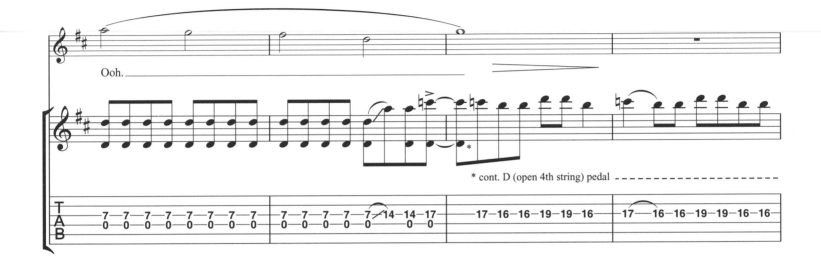

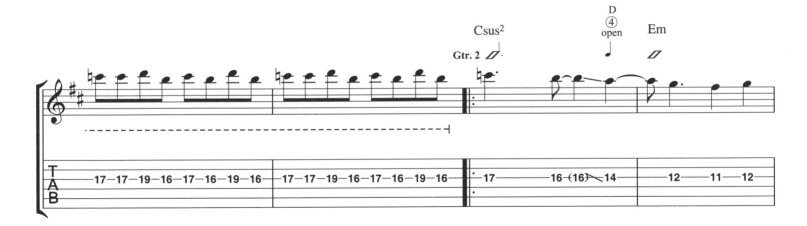

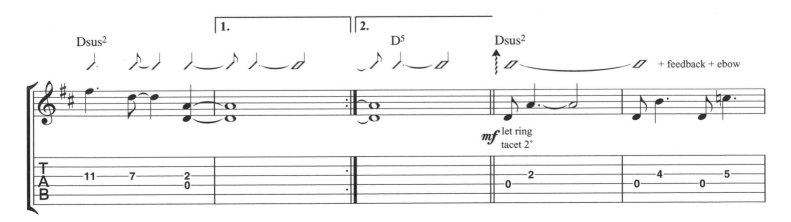

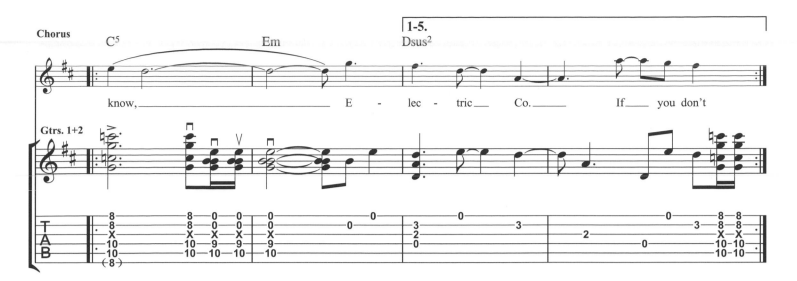

know,_____ E - lec - tric__ Co.____ If__ you don't

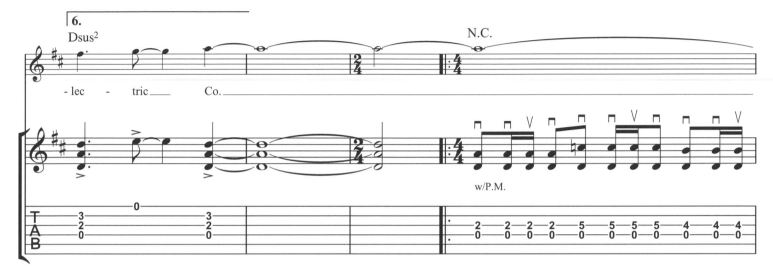

- lec - tric__ Co._____

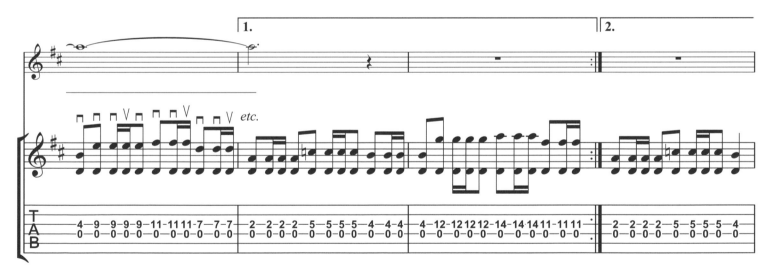

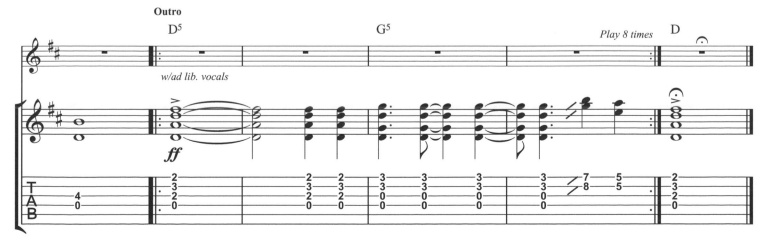

Gloria

Words & Music by U2

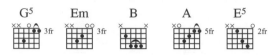

Tune all guitars down a semitone

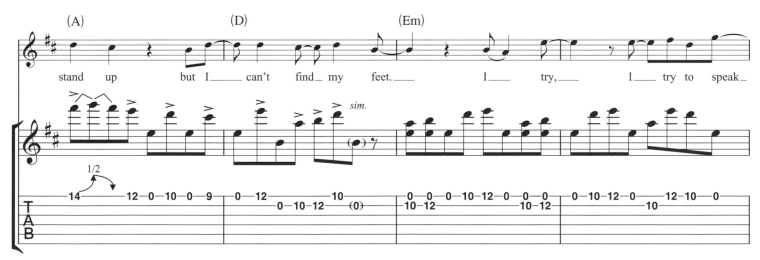

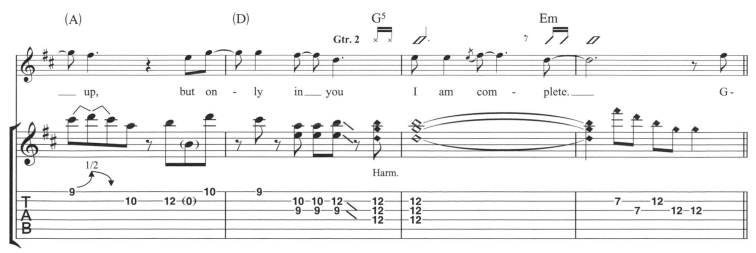

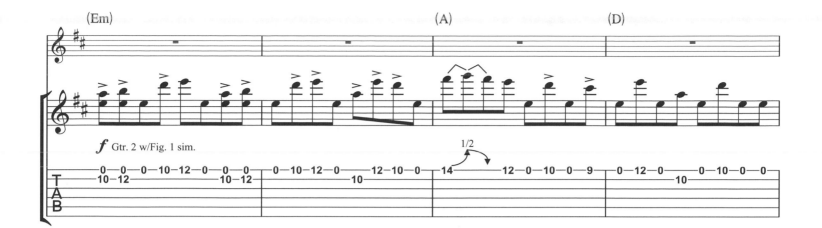

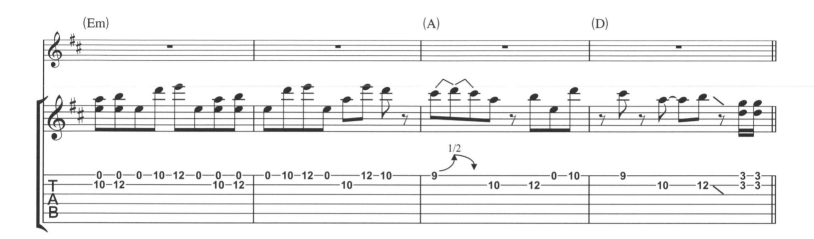

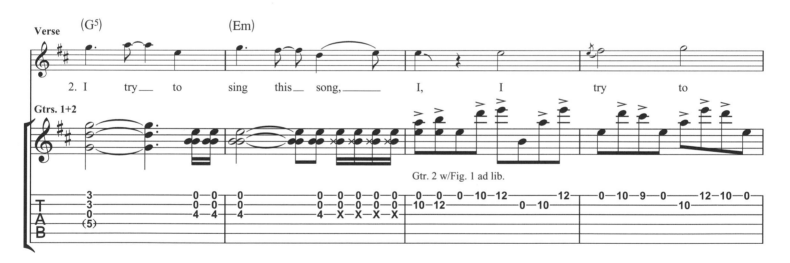

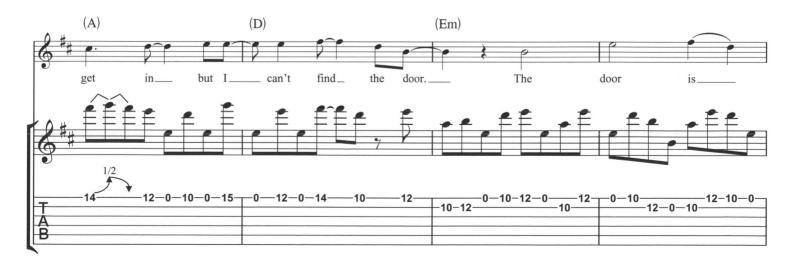

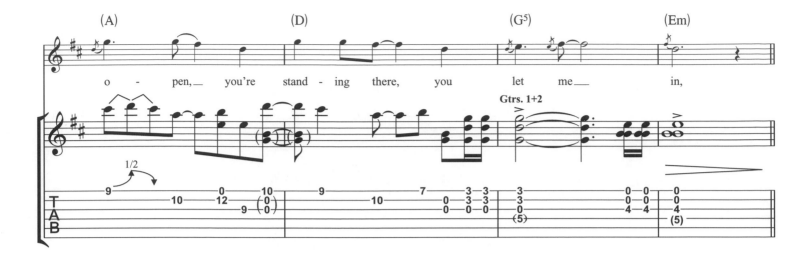

o - pen,___ you're stand - ing there, you let me___ in,

Gtrs. 1+2

1/2

Chorus

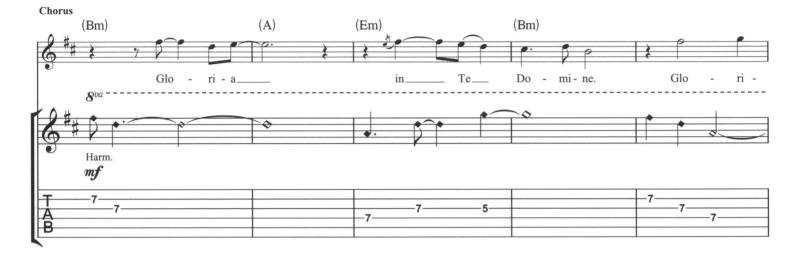

Glo - ri - a___ in___ Te___ Do - mi - ne. Glo - ri -

8va

Harm.

mf

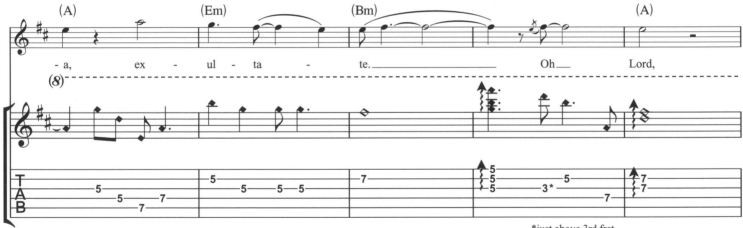

- a, ex - ul - ta - te.___ Oh___ Lord,

(8)

*just above 3rd fret

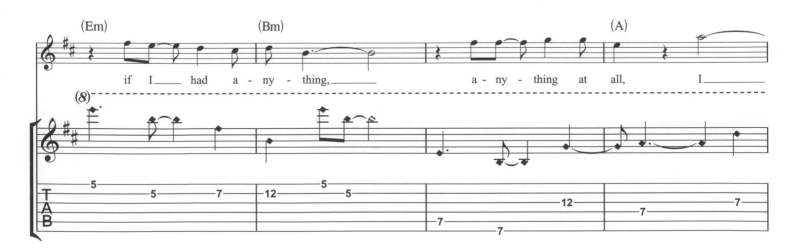

if I___ had a - ny - thing,___ a - ny - thing at all, I___

(8)

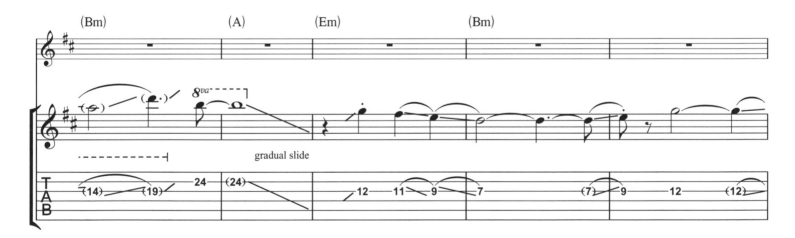

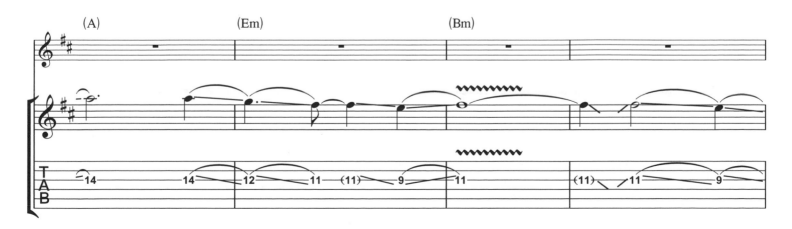

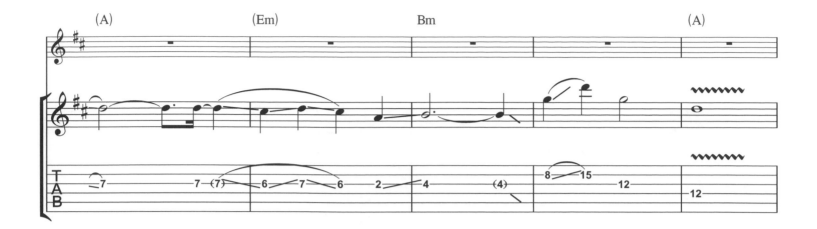

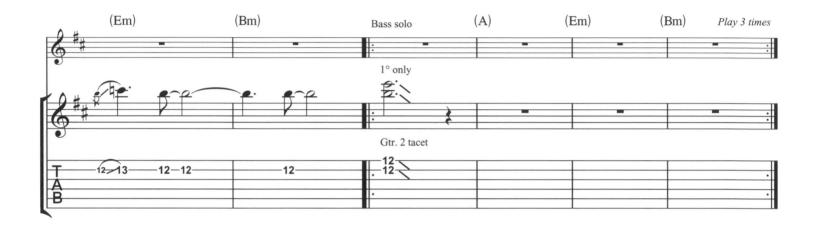

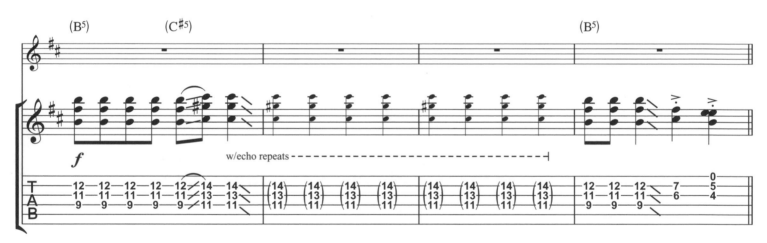

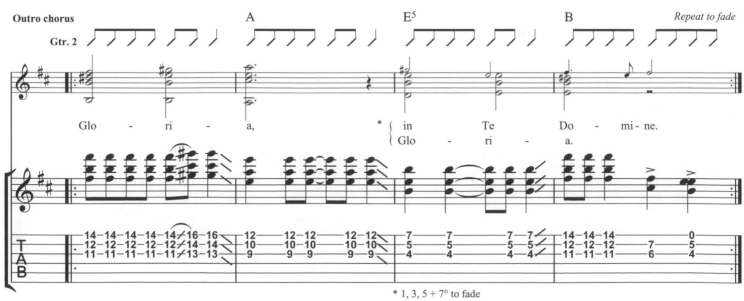

Sunday Bloody Sunday

Words & Music by U2

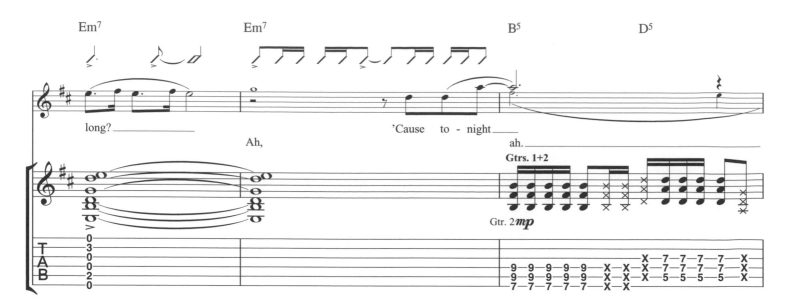

long? _____ 'Cause to - night _____ ah. _____
Ah,

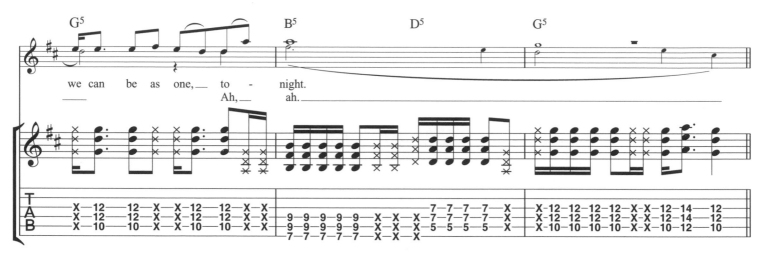

we can be as one, ____ to - night. _____
Ah, ____ ah. _____

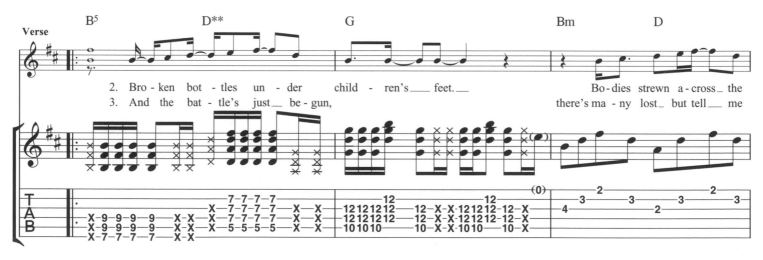

Verse

2. Bro - ken bot - tles un - der child - ren's ___ feet. ___ Bo - dies strewn a - cross __ the
3. And the bat - tle's just __ be - gun, there's ma - ny lost __ but tell __ me

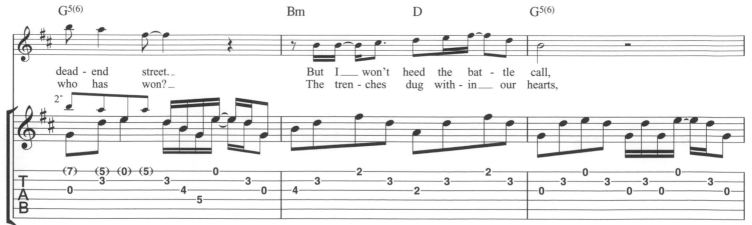

dead - end street. __ But I __ won't heed the bat - tle call,
who has won? __ The tren - ches dug with - in __ our hearts,

34

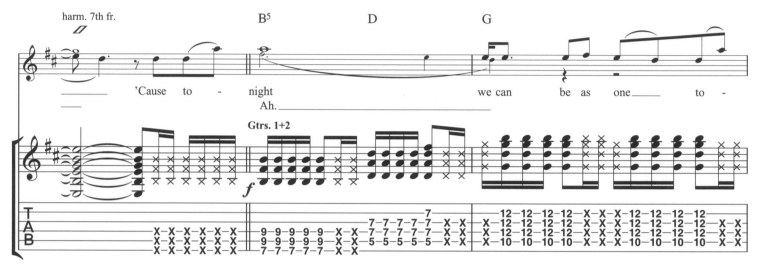

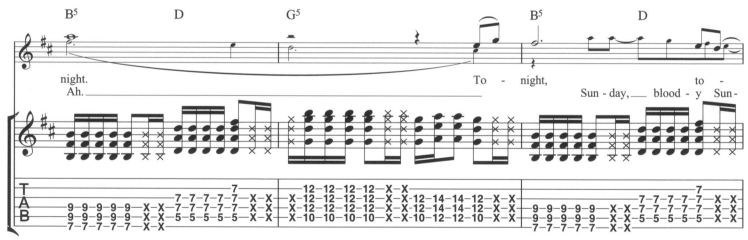

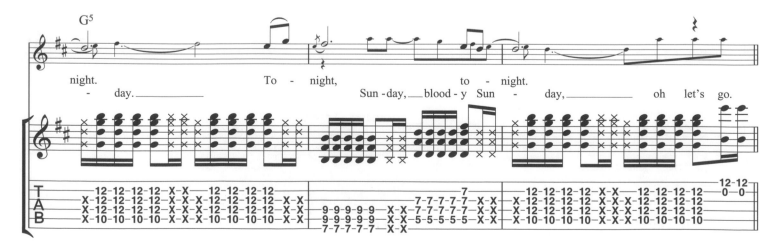

Solo

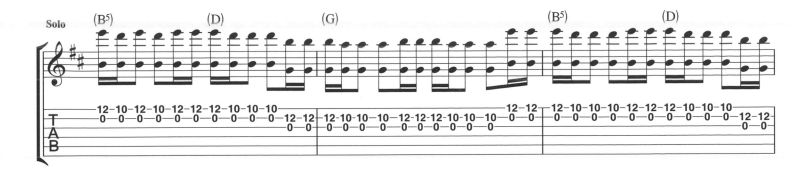

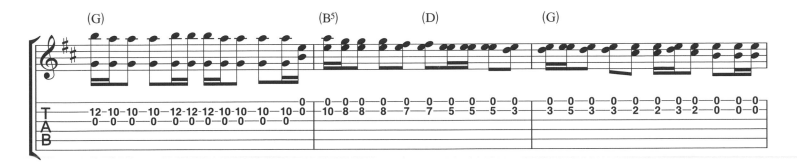

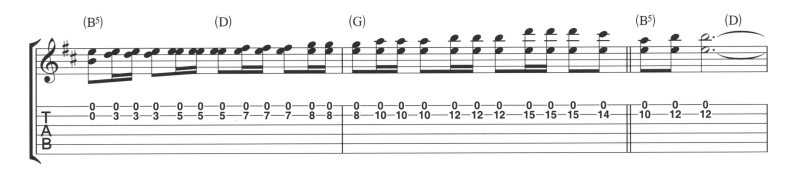

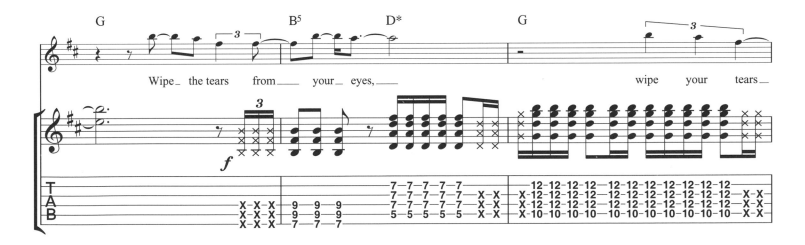

Wipe the tears from your eyes, wipe your tears

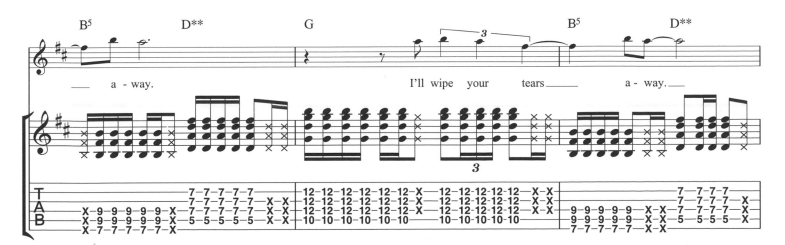

a - way. I'll wipe your tears a - way.

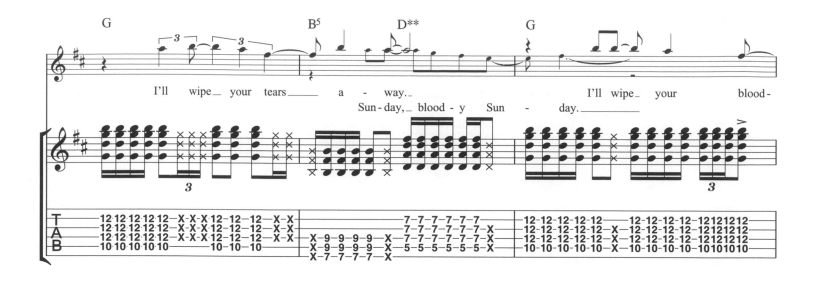

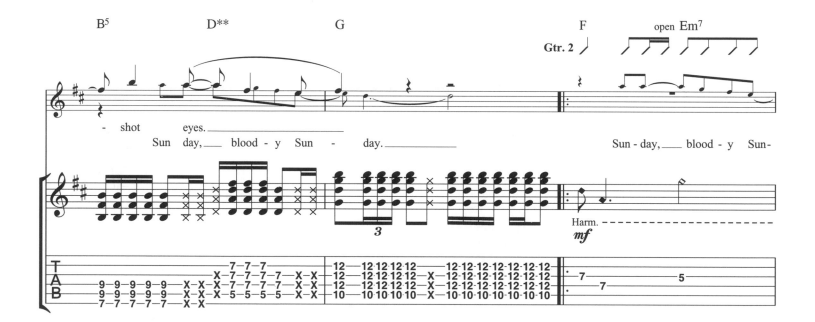

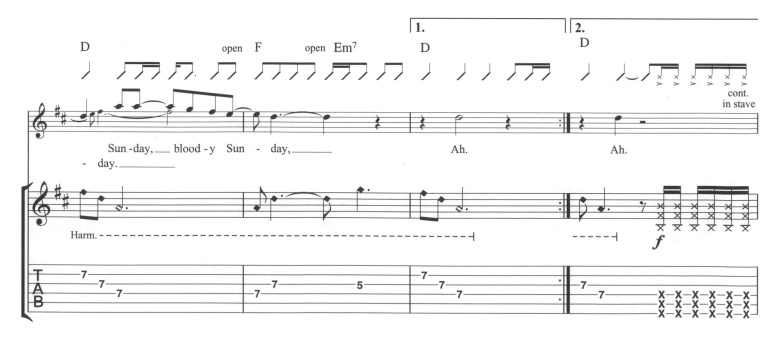

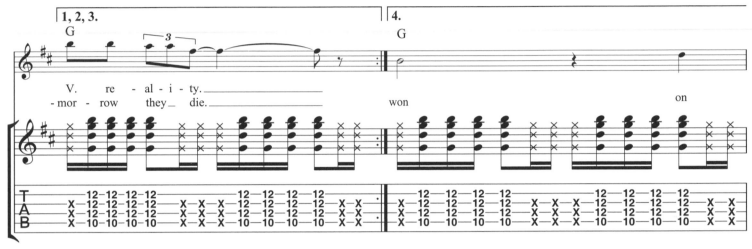

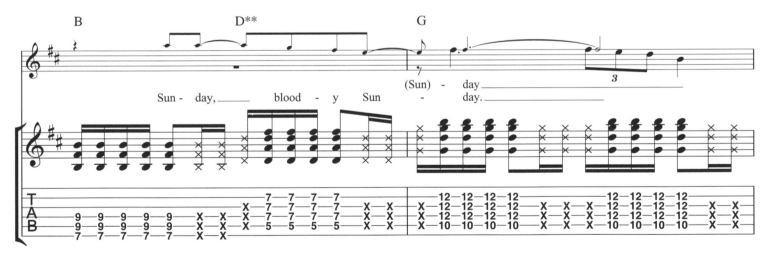

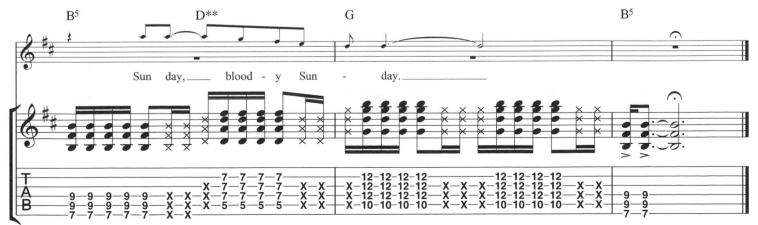

New Year's Day

Words & Music by U2

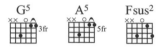

Tune all guitars down a semitone

Intro

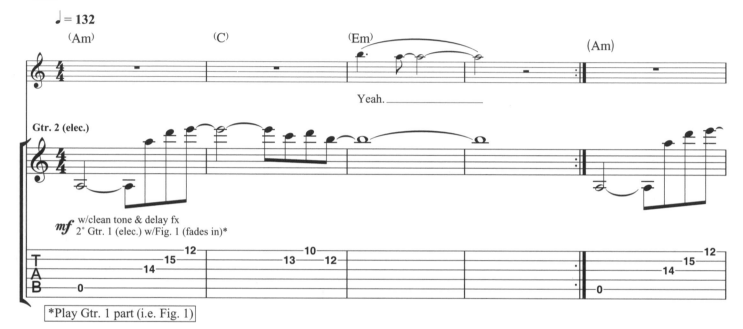

*Play Gtr. 1 part (i.e. Fig. 1)

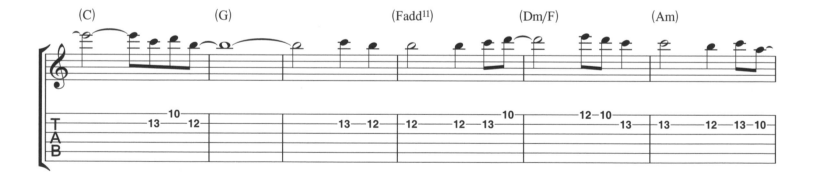

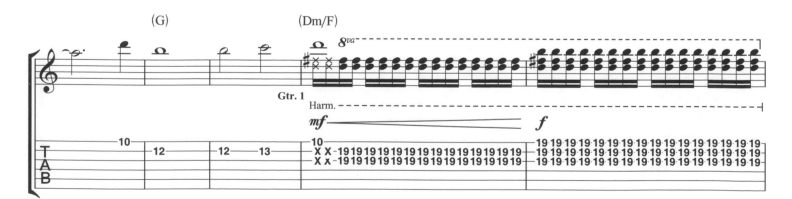

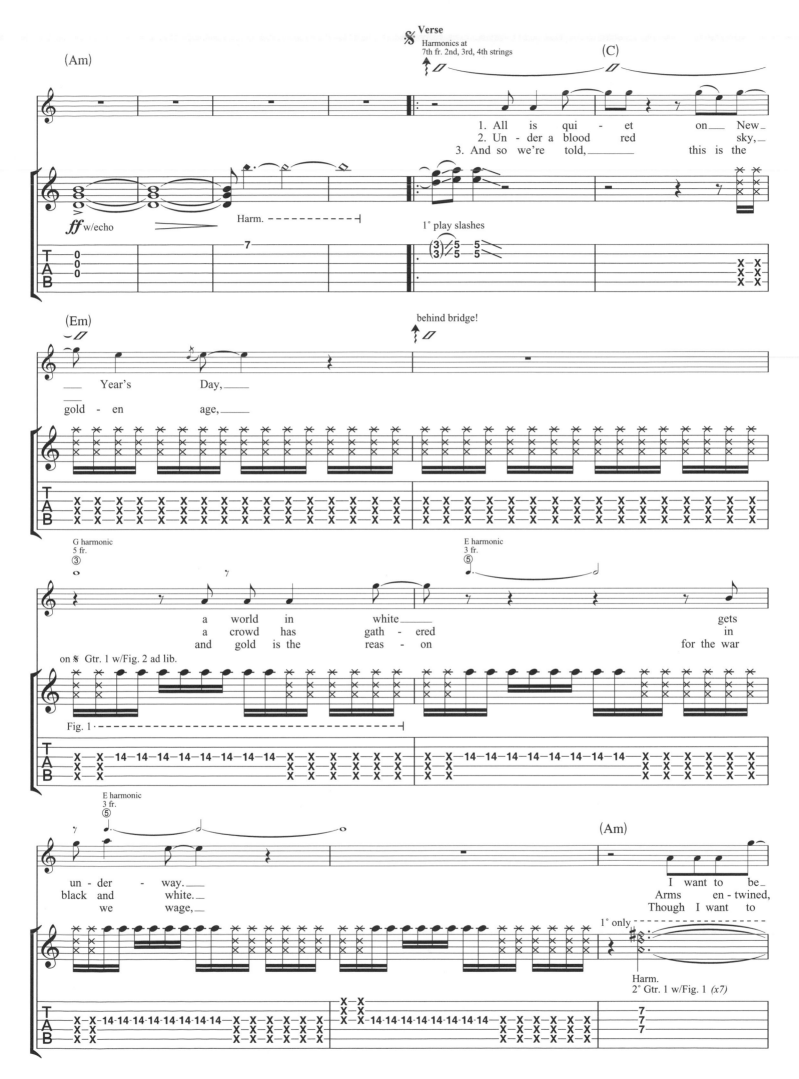

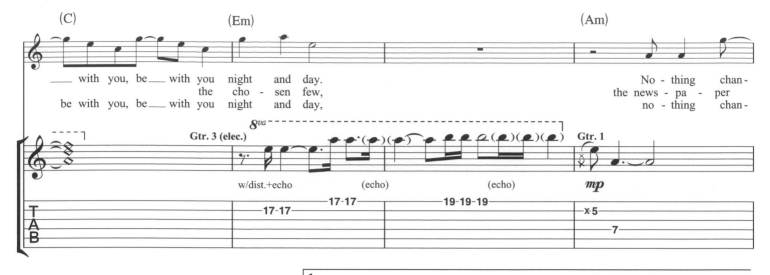

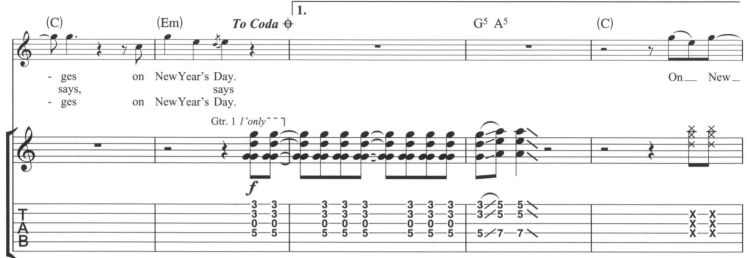

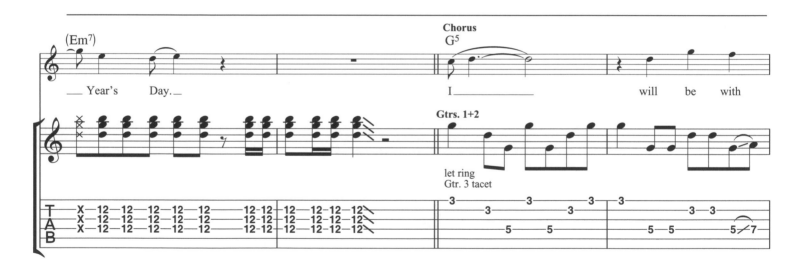

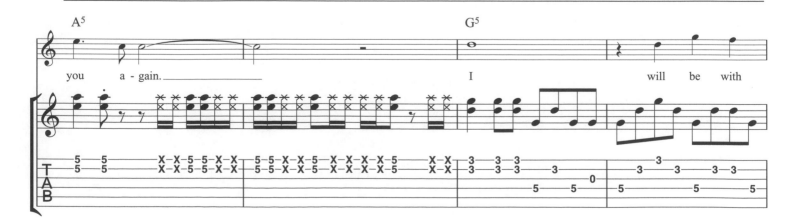

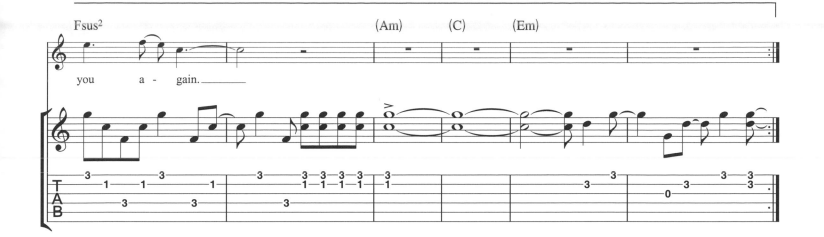

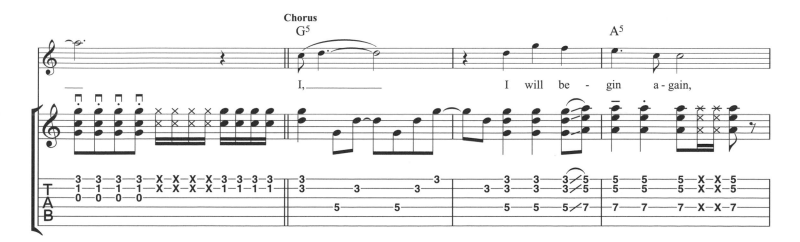

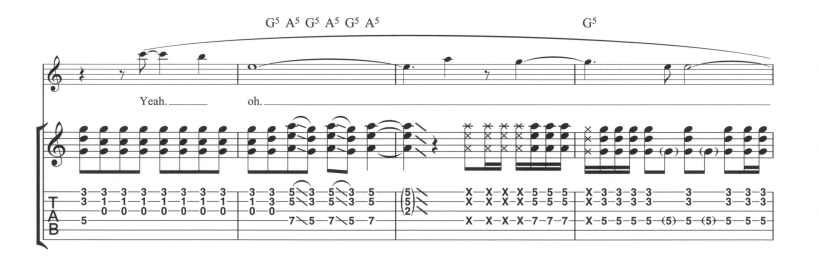

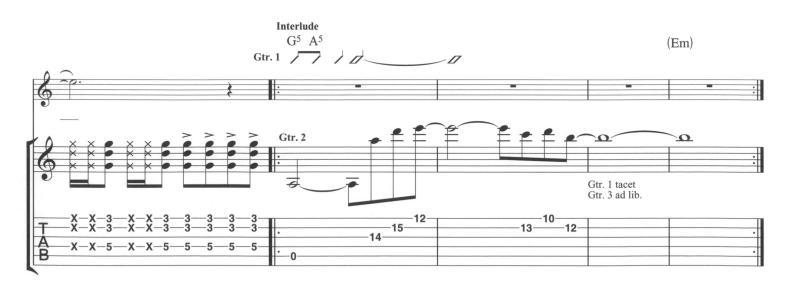

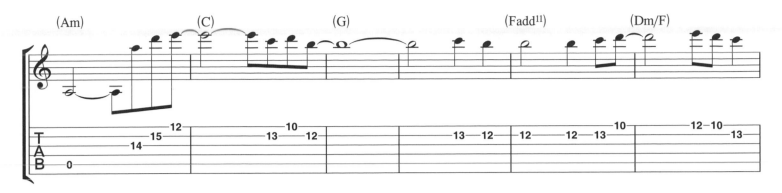

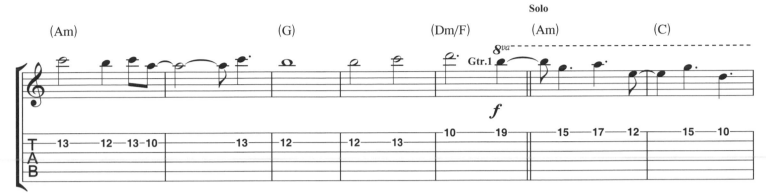

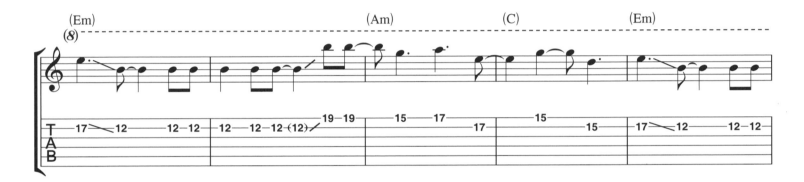

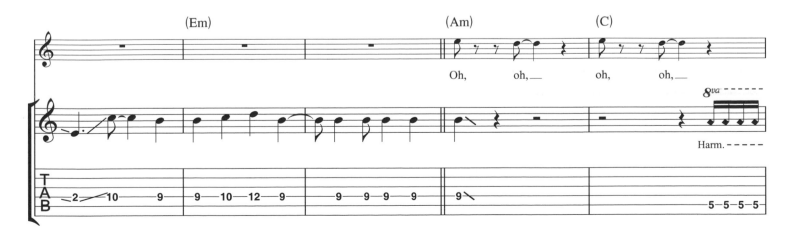

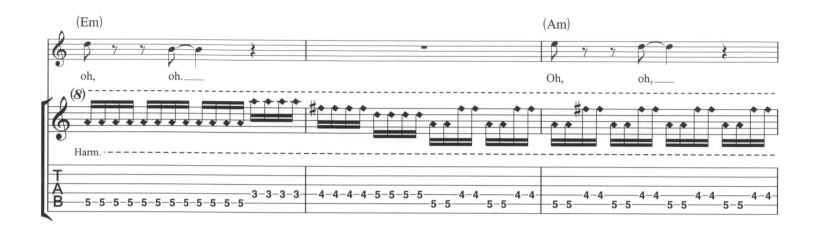

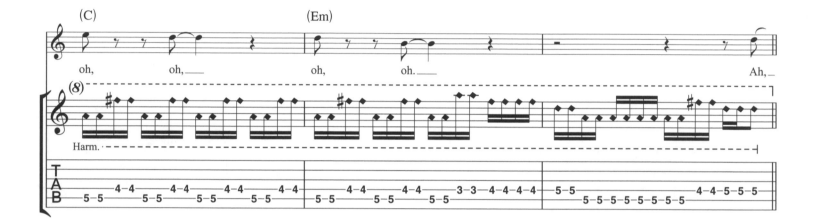

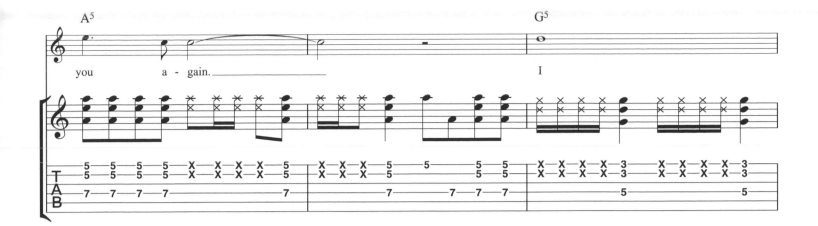

you   a - gain._____   I

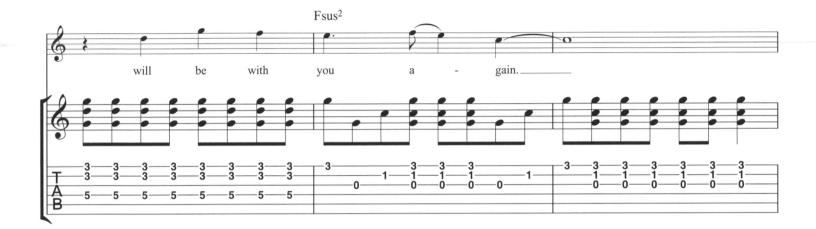

will   be   with   you   a -   gain._____

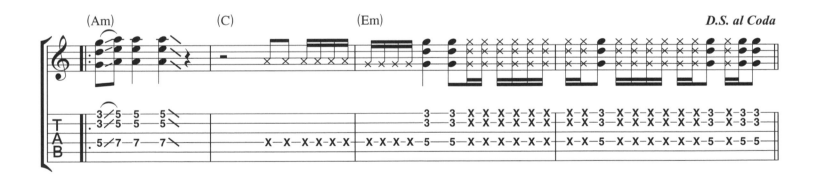

D.S. al Coda

(Am)   (C)   (Em)

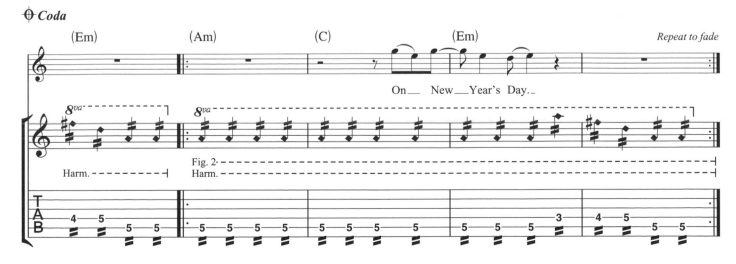

𝄌 *Coda*

(Em)   (Am)   (C)   (Em)   *Repeat to fade*

On___ New ___Year's Day.___

Two Hearts Beat As One

Words & Music by U2

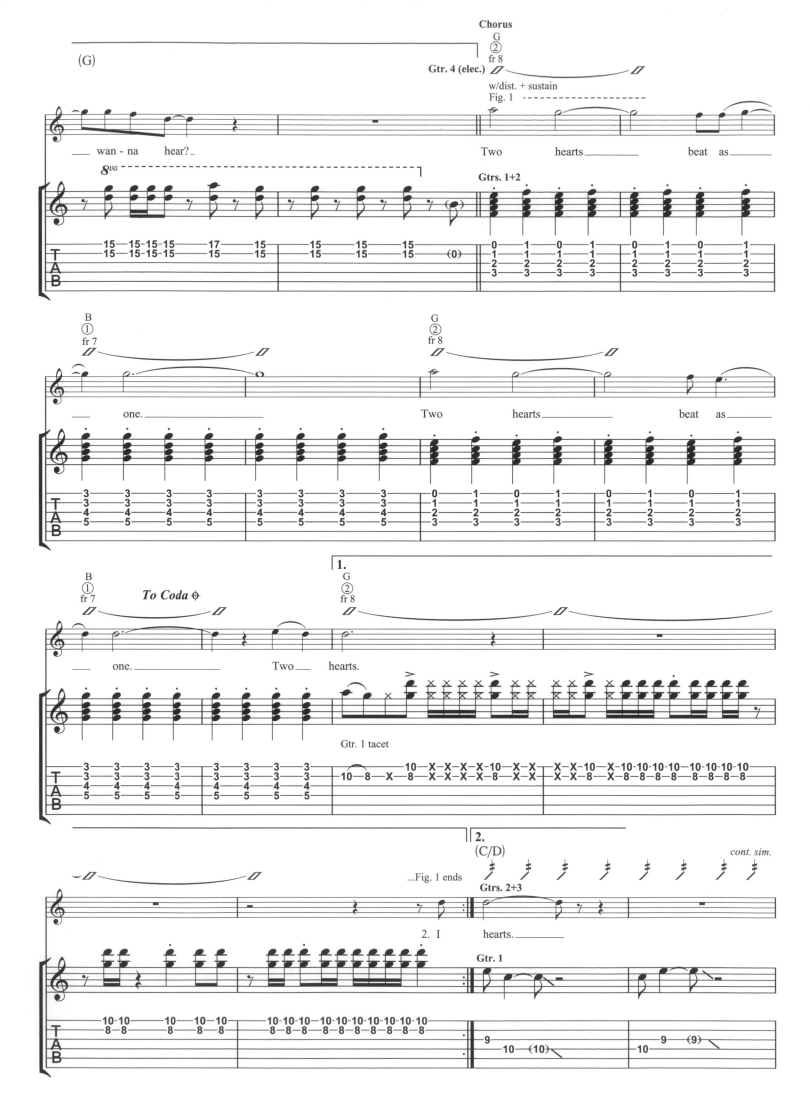

Beat on black, beat on white, beat on a - ny - thing, don't get it right. Beat on you, beat on me, beat

on love.

Gtr. 2

w/percussive ♪ rhythm.
Gtr. 1 tacet
Gtr. 3 plays perc. rhythm only

D.S. al Coda

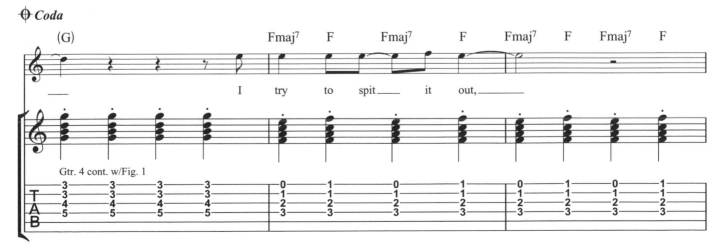

⊕ *Coda*

I   try   to   spit___   it   out,___

Gtr. 4 cont. w/Fig. 1

try to ex-plain_____ the way I wan-na feel._____

_____ Oh, yeah._____ Two_____ hearts.

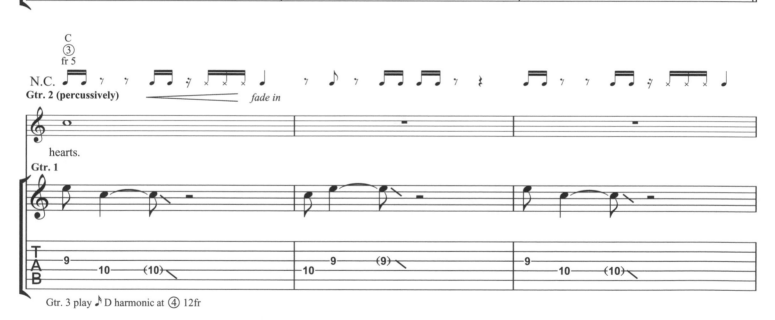

Gtr. 2 (percussively)
fade in

Gtr. 1

Gtr. 3 play D harmonic at ④ 12fr

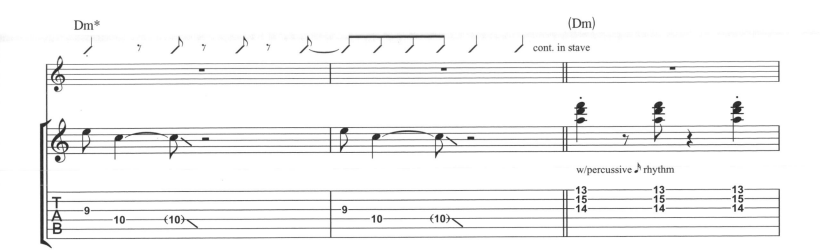

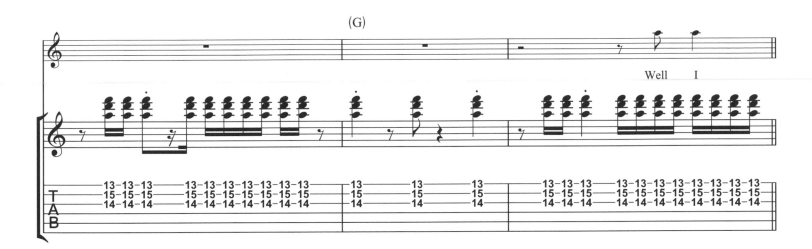

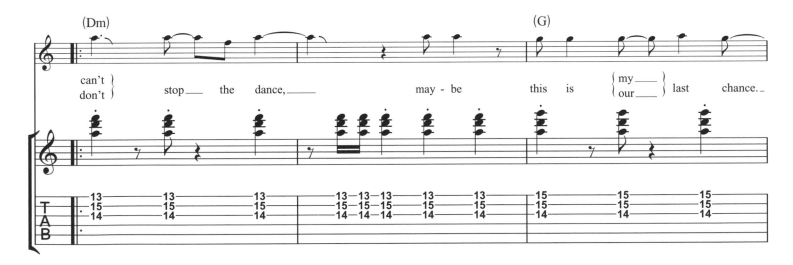

Guitar Tablature Explained

Guitar music can be notated in three different ways: on a musical stave, in tablature, and in rhythm slashes.

RHYTHM SLASHES are written above the stave. Strum chords in the rhythm indicated. Round noteheads indicate single notes.

THE MUSICAL STAVE shows pitches and rhythms and is divided by lines into bars. Pitches are named after the first seven letters of the alphabet.

TABLATURE graphically represents the guitar fingerboard. Each horizontal line represents a string, and each number represents a fret.

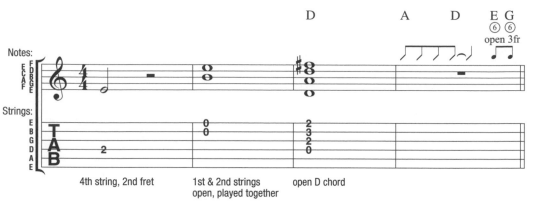

4th string, 2nd fret   1st & 2nd strings open, played together   open D chord

Definitions For Special Guitar Notation

SEMI-TONE BEND: Strike the note and bend up a semi-tone (1/2 step).

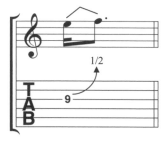

WHOLE-TONE BEND: Strike the note and bend up a whole-tone (whole step).

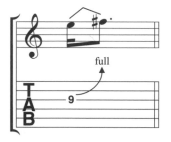

GRACE NOTE BEND: Strike the note and bend as indicated. Play the first note as quickly as possible.

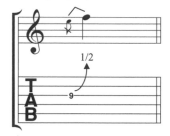

QUARTER-TONE BEND: Strike the note and bend up a 1/4 step.

BEND & RELEASE: Strike the note and bend up as indicated, then release back to the original note.

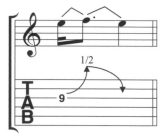

COMPOUND BEND & RELEASE: Strike the note and bend up and down in the rhythm indicated.

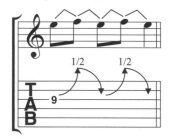

PRE-BEND: Bend the note as indicated, then strike it.

PRE-BEND & RELEASE: Bend the note as indicated. Strike it and release the note back to the original pitch.

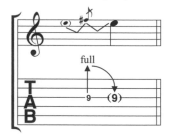

UNISON BEND: Strike the two notes simultaneously and bend the lower note up to the pitch of the higher.

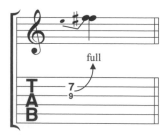

BEND & RESTRIKE: Strike the note and bend as indicated then restrike the string where the symbol occurs.

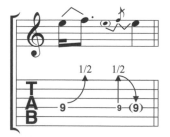

BEND, HOLD AND RELEASE: Same as bend and release but hold the bend for the duration of the tie.

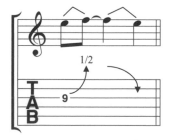

BEND AND TAP: Bend the note as indicated and tap the higher fret while still holding the bend.

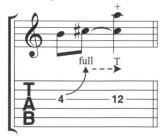

VIBRATO: The string is vibrated by rapidly bending and releasing the note with the fretting hand.

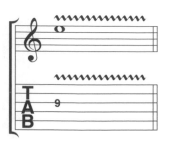

HAMMER-ON: Strike the first note with one finger, then sound the second note (on the same string) with another finger by fretting it without picking.

PULL-OFF: Place both fingers on the notes to be sounded, strike the first note and without picking, pull the finger off to sound the second note.

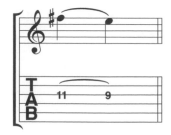

LEGATO SLIDE (GLISS): Strike the first note and then slide the same fret-hand finger up or down to the second note. The second note is not struck.

NOTE: The speed of any bend is indicated by the music notation and tempo.

SHIFT SLIDE (GLISS & RESTRIKE): Same as legato slide, except the second note is struck.

TRILL: Very rapidly alternate between the notes indicated by continuously hammering on and pulling off.

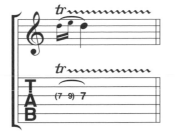

TAPPING: Hammer ("tap") the fret indicated with the pick-hand index or middle finger and pull off to the note fretted by the fret hand.

PICK SCRAPE: The edge of the pick is rubbed down (or up) the string, producing a scratchy sound.

MUFFLED STRINGS: A percussive sound is produced by laying the fret hand across the string(s) without depressing, and striking them with the pick hand.

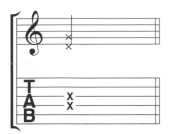

NATURAL HARMONIC: Strike the note while the fret-hand lightly touches the string directly over the fret indicated.

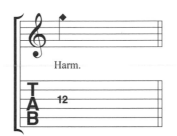

PINCH HARMONIC: The note is fretted normally and a harmonic is produced by adding the edge of the thumb or the tip of the index finger of the pick hand to the normal pick attack.

HARP HARMONIC: The note is fretted normally and a harmonic is produced by gently resting the pick hand's index finger directly above the indicated fret (in brackets) while plucking the appropriate string.

PALM MUTING: The note is partially muted by the pick hand lightly touching the string(s) just before the bridge.

RAKE: Drag the pick across the strings indicated with a single motion.

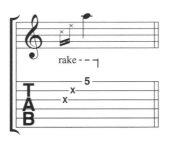

TREMOLO PICKING: The note is picked as rapidly and continuously as possible.

ARPEGGIATE: Play the notes of the chord indicated by quickly rolling them from bottom to top.

SWEEP PICKING: Rhythmic downstroke and/or upstroke motion across the strings.

VIBRATO DIVE BAR AND RETURN: The pitch of the note or chord is dropped a specific number of steps (in rhythm) then returned to the original pitch.

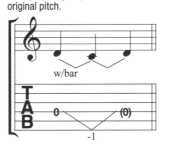

VIBRATO BAR SCOOP: Depress the bar just before striking the note, then quickly release the bar.

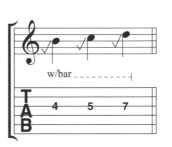

VIBRATO BAR DIP: Strike the note and then immediately drop a specific number of steps, then release back to the original pitch.

additional musical definitions

(accent)	• Accentuate note (play it louder).	
(accent)	• Accentuate note with great intensity.	
(staccato)	• Shorten time value of note.	
⊓	• Downstroke	
V	• Upstroke	

NOTE: Tablature numbers in brackets mean:
1. The note is sustained, but a new articulation (such as hammer on or slide) begins.
2. A note may be fretted but not necessarily played.

D.%. al Coda
• Go back to the sign (%), then play until the bar marked ***To Coda*** ⊕ then skip to the section marked ⊕ ***Coda***.

D.C. al Fine
• Go back to the beginning of the song and play until the bar marked ***Fine***.

tacet
• Instrument is silent (drops out).

• Repeat bars between signs.

|1. |2.
• When a repeated section has different endings, play the first ending only the first time and the second ending only the second time.

1 2 3 4 5 6 7 8 9

CD Track Listing

Full instrumental performances (with guitar)...

1 Out Of Control
2 I Will Follow
3 The Electric Co.
4 Gloria
5 Sunday Bloody Sunday
6 New Year's Day
7 Two Hearts Beat As One

Backing tracks only (without guitar)...

8 Out Of Control
9 I Will Follow
10 The Electric Co.
11 Gloria
12 Sunday Bloody Sunday
13 New Year's Day
14 Two Hearts Beat As One

All tracks:
(U2) Blue Mountain Music Limited.

To remove your CD from the plastic sleeve, lift the
small lip on the side to break the perforated strip.
Replace the disc after use for convenient storage.